ORDINARY PEOPLE CHANGE the WORLD

I am
Amelia Earhart

BRAD MELTZER

illustrated by Christopher Eliopoulos

DIAL BOOKS FOR YOUNG READERS an imprint of Penguin Group (USA) LLC

For Lila,
my daughter,
who makes me feel
like I'm soaring

—B.M.

For Audra.
My Life,
My Co-pilot,
My Hero
—C.E.

I am **Amelia Earhart.**

When I was little, people told me that girls should wear dresses and play with dolls.

They said we shouldn't have "unladylike" adventures.

I didn't agree.

In fact, when I was seven years old, my sister and I decided to build our own roller coaster in our backyard. We placed two planks of wood up against the side of our tool shed.

The cab was a wooden packing box with roller-skate wheels attached to the bottom. We greased the wood with lard so we'd move super-fast.

Of course, I got to ride first.
This was my moment.

I still remember the wind in my face.

My stomach seemed to sink.

The crash was loud and
noisy and messy.
It certainly wasn't ladylike.
But it was awesome!

It wasn't the last time
I would fly.
As I got older, I went to
many air shows.

When I was twenty-three years old (but still a kid at heart), my dad took me to meet Frank Hawks, a man who would eventually set many of his own flight records.

For ten dollars, Hawks agreed to take me on my very first flight.

For ten minutes, we flew through
the sky and out over the Pacific Ocean.
By the time I was two or three hundred
feet off the ground, I knew one thing:
I had to fly.

To save for my flying lessons, I worked as a truck driver (which wasn't ladylike either) . . .

a stenographer (which is a fancy-schmancy word for someone who writes down what people say) . . .

and even a photographer.

But here's my secret: I wasn't a natural.
I wasn't the best pilot.
I just worked harder than anyone else.

Most important, like that day on the roller coaster,
I dared to do what so many said couldn't be done.

I became the first woman to fly across the Atlantic Ocean—and then the first woman to fly *by myself* across the Atlantic.

Back then, people took boats to get to Europe, sailing for weeks. Planes were still a new thing. In fact, on the day I took off, one magazine ran an article that said women would never be able to fly that far.

But *I* did.

To do it, I had to fly for fourteen hours and fifty-
six minutes with no rest, no break. Sometimes the sun
was so blinding, I could barely see where I was going.

In the process, I also broke the record for crossing the ocean in the shortest time, doing it faster than any man or woman ever.

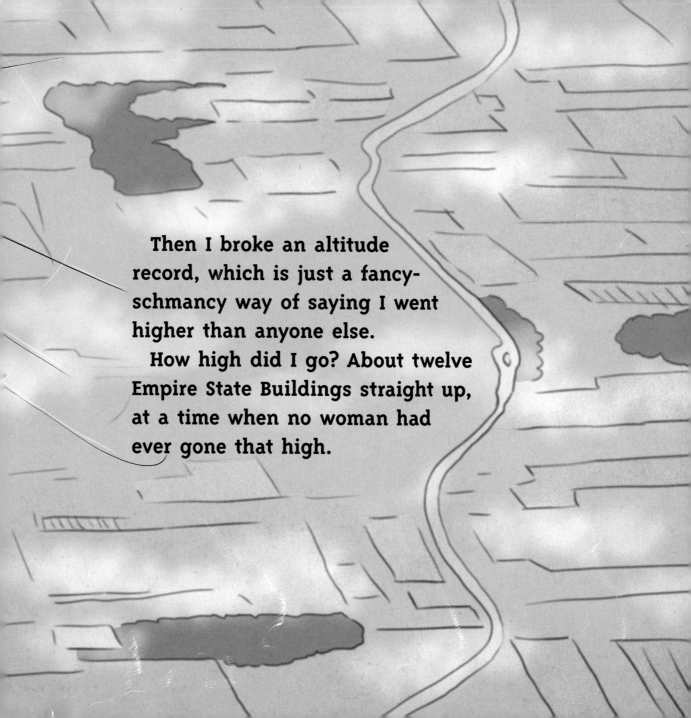

Then I broke an altitude record, which is just a fancy-schmancy way of saying I went higher than anyone else.

How high did I go? About twelve Empire State Buildings straight up, at a time when no woman had ever gone that high.

In my life, I took many flights.

Every single time, there was someone
who said that I wouldn't be able to do it.

Never let anyone stop you.
Whatever your dream is, chase it.
Work hard for it.
You will find it.
It is the best lesson I can give you.

I am Amelia Earhart.
I know no bounds.
And I hope you'll remember that the greatest flight you'll ever take, is the one no one has tried before.

"Never interrupt someone
doing what you said couldn't
be done."

—AMELIA EARHART

Amelia, age 7

Amelia in the cockpit, 1936

Amelia with her
first plane, the Kinner
Airster biplane, which
she named *Canary*

Frank Hawks, pilot
who first took Amelia
on an airplane ride

Neta Snook, Amelia's
flight instructor

DIAL BOOKS FOR YOUNG READERS
Published by the Penguin Group • Penguin Group (USA) LLC, 375 Hudson Street, New York, New York 10014

USA | Canada | UK | Ireland | Australia | New Zealand | India | South Africa | China
penguin.com

A PENGUIN RANDOM HOUSE COMPANY

Text copyright © 2014 by Brad Meltzer • Illustrations copyright © 2014 by Christopher Eliopoulos

Library of Congress Cataloging-in-Publication Data
Meltzer, Brad. • I am Amelia Earhart/Brad Meltzer; illustrated by Christopher Eliopoulos. • pages cm. — (Ordinary people change the world)
ISBN 978-0-8037-4082-2 (hardcover) • 1. Earhart, Amelia, 1897–1937—Juvenile literature. 2. Women air pilots—United States—Biography—Juvenile literature.
3. Air pilots—United States—Biography—Juvenile literature. I. Eliopoulos, Christopher, illustrator. II. Title. • TL540.E3M45 2014 629.13092—dc23 [B] 2013010559

Amelia on page 36 and young Amelia on page 38 photos courtesy of Getty Images • Amelia photo on page 38 (bottom) and Neta Snook photo on page 39 private collection of Karsten Smedal, courtesy of Ames Historical Society • Amelia in cockpit photo on page 38 courtesy of Purdue University • Frank Hawks photo on page 39 courtesy of San Diego Air & Space Museum

Manufactured in the USA on acid-free paper • 10 9 8 7 6 5 4 3 2
Designed by Jason Henry • Text set in Triplex • The artwork for this book was created digitally.